THE PRINCE AND THE PAUPER

by
Mark Twain

Teacher Guide

Written by
Pat Watson

Edited by
Katherine E. Martinez

Note

The Tor paperback edition of the book, published by Tom Doherty Associates, LLC, ©1992 was used to prepare this guide. The page references may differ in other editions.

Please note: Please assess the appropriateness of this book for the age level and maturity of your students prior to reading and discussing it with your class.

ISBN 1-58130-766-7

To order, contact your local school supply store, or—

Novel Units, Inc.
P.O. Box 97
Bulverde, TX 78163-0097

Web site: www.educyberstor.com

Table of Contents

Skills and Strategies

Thinking
Compare/contrast, analysis,
brainstorming

Writing
Poetry, eulogy, letter,
characterization, TV script

Listening/Speaking
Discussion, oral reports

Comprehension
Cause/effect, predictions,
analysis, application

Vocabulary
Target words, definitions

Literary Elements
Characterization, simile,
metaphor, plot
development, setting,
theme, irony, genre

Across the Curriculum
Music—folk tune,
appropriate background
music; Art—caricature,
drawing, montage

Genre: fiction; satire

Setting: England, 1547

Date: first published in 1881

Point of View: third-person omniscient

Themes: loyalty, monarchy vs. democracy, mistaken identity

Protagonists: Tom Canty; Edward Tudor

Antagonists: established English customs; society's class system; abusive father

Style: narrative

Summary

A young beggar, Tom Canty, and the Prince of Wales, Edward Tudor, accidentally discover they are identical except for their clothes. On a sudden whim, they exchange clothes, and each is plunged into a world for which he is not prepared: Tom as the pampered future King of England; Edward as the mistreated son of a thief. When no one will believe Tom when he tries to explain what has happened, he is forced to adapt to the protocol of court life in the role of the Prince of Wales. No one believes Edward's protests that he is the king's son, and he struggles to survive in London's dark world of evil. After King Henry VIII dies, the destiny of each of the boys hinges on whether or not they can convince someone to believe the truth. Their experiences in these assumed roles will forever change their lives.

About the Author

Personal: Samuel Langhorne Clemens (Mark Twain) was born November 30, 1835, in Florida, Missouri. In 1839, the family moved to Hannibal, a town on the Mississippi River. Twain took his first job, a printer's apprentice for a newspaper and printing firm, after his father died in 1847, leaving unpaid debts. In 1852, he assisted his older brother, Orion, at the Hannibal *Journal*. He later traveled extensively and worked at a variety of occupations, including typesetter, apprenticed steamboat pilot, prospector, and journalist. In his later years, he traveled extensively as a lecturer. He married Olivia "Livy" Langdon in 1870. Of their four children, Langdon, Susy, Clara, and Jean, only Clara outlived him. He died of heart disease on April 21, 1910.

Writing Career: Clemens first used the pen name Mark Twain in 1863. In 1865, his first story, "The Celebrated Jumping Frog of Calaveras County," was published. The publication of *The Innocents Abroad* (1868) began a long period of literary acclaim and financial prosperity. In addition to *The Prince and the Pauper* (1881), other noted works include *Roughing It* (1872), *The Gilded Age* (1873),

The Adventures of Tom Sawyer (1876), *A Tramp Abroad* (1880), *Life on the Mississippi* (1883), *The Adventures of Huckleberry Finn* (1884), *A Connecticut Yankee in King Arthur's Court* (1889), and *Puddn'head Wilson* (1894). Although he gained acclaim as a writer, Twain invested in several unsuccessful business ventures, and he declared bankruptcy in 1893. To offset his financial losses, he began traveling and speaking.

Background Information

Mark Twain wrote *The Prince and the Pauper* after setting aside the unfinished manuscript for *The Adventures of Huckleberry Finn*. He hoped to extend his reading audience to more children and to prove that he could write a precise, refined, and tasteful humorous novel. He succeeded in both goals, and the novel was acclaimed by the general public and by literary critics. In addition, the novel presents the pageantry of the British monarchy and the plight of England's common man.

Teaching Strategies

The novel is adaptable for different grade levels and can be presented as an adventure tale of mistaken identity, or as a satire that reflects Twain's aversion to the injustices of the British monarchy and its cruel treatment of the common man. He portrays the severity of the laws of that era by having Edward, the King, experience some of the unjust penalties and by having him see other injustices applied to English subjects. Twain's references to the religious and political biases of 16th century England correlate in many ways with his views of the Blue Laws of Connecticut, the first printed laws of that colony. Samuel Peters publicized these laws in a book, *A General History of Connecticut* (1781). Some of the most famous laws include: No Priest shall abide in this Dominion; he shall be banished, and suffer death on his return. No one shall read Common-Prayer, keep Christmas on Saints-days, make minced pies, dance, play cards, or play on any instrument of music, except the drum, trumpet, and jawharp. Every male shall have his hair cut round according to a cap. No one shall travel, cook victuals, make beds, sweep house, cut hair, or shave, on the Sabbath Day.

Historical Background
(People and events portrayed in the novel)

House of Tudor: England's ruling family from 1485 to 1603, beginning with Henry VII. He restored order to England after several years of civil unrest.

Henry VIII (1491–1547) continued Henry VII's work toward unifying England. Because of his divorces and subsequent remarriages, Henry VIII broke all ties between England and the Roman Catholic Church, making the monarch head of the Church of England. His wives included Catherine of Aragon, Anne Boleyn, Jane Seymour, Anne of Cleves, Catherine Howard, and Catherine Parr, who outlived him.

Edward VI, Prince of Wales, (1537–1553) was the son of Jane Seymour. He succeeded his father, Henry VIII, in 1547, when he was nine years old. His uncle, Edward Seymour, Duke of Somerset, governed for him. Edward died of tuberculosis when he was sixteen years old. Desiring to keep England Protestant, Edward named his cousin Lady Jane Grey, a Protestant, as his successor.

Lady Jane Grey (1537–1554), known as the "nine-day queen," became Queen of England July 10, 1553. On July 19, the claims to the throne of Edward's half-sister, Mary, were recognized. Lady Jane was charged with high treason and imprisoned in the Tower of London. Mary ordered her beheaded on February 12, 1554.

Mary I (1516–1558), daughter of Henry VIII and Catherine of Aragon, was Queen of England from 1553 until her death in 1558. A devout Roman Catholic, she attempted to return England to the Roman Catholic Church. She became known as "Bloody Mary" because of the persecutions of Protestants under her reign. She was succeeded by her half-sister, Elizabeth, a Protestant.

Elizabeth I (1533–1603), daughter of Henry VIII and Anne Boleyn, reigned from 1558 until her death in 1603. A Protestant, she again made England independent of the Roman Catholic Church and strengthened the Church of England. Her reign is often called England's "Golden Age." She never married, thereby leaving no immediate heir. After her death, King James VI of Scotland, great-grandson of Henvy VII's oldest daughter, became England's first Stuart king, ending the rule of the House of Tudor.

The Tower of London is a group of stone buildings on the north bank of the Thames River. Dating from the late 1000s, it has served as a fortress, a prison, and a palace. It has been the site of imprisonment of many famous people, including Lady Jane Grey, who was beheaded there. Today, the Tower is primarily a showplace and museum, containing crowns, scepters, and other treasures of English royalty.

The London Bridge was the only bridge over the Thames until 1750; it was torn down in 1831. The heads of executed traitors were displayed over the entrances of houses that originally lined both sides of the bridge.

Punch and Judy are the main characters in a comic puppet show popular in England. These shows had a great deal of rough, violent humor. The allusion to Punch and Judy shows (p. 12) is an anachronism because they were not introduced into England until 1662.

Stone of Scone, a.k.a. Stone of Destiny, is the sandstone block on which kings of Scotland were crowned until 1296. Edward I brought the stone to England and incorporated it as part of the coronation chair in Westminster Abbey. In 1996, Queen Elizabeth authorized its return to Scotland, to be brought back to England temporarily when a British monarch is crowned.

Characters

Tom Canty: unwanted at birth; nine years old; abused and forced to beg by his father; educated by a priest; destined to a life of poverty; dreams of seeing a "real" prince

Edward Tudor (Prince of Wales): all England rejoiced at his birth; nine years old; pampered son of King Henry VIII and Jane Seymour; destined to become a king

Tom's family:
John Canty: Tom's cruel, abusive father; a thief

His mother: kind, concerned about Tom; shares her meager food with him

His grandmother: John's mother; cruel and abusive; a beggar

Nan and Bet: his twin sisters; dirty, unkempt; forced to beg

Edward's family and members of the court:
Henry VIII: King of England; ill; dreaded by his subjects; a loving, doting father

Elizabeth: his half-sister; kind and loving

Lady Jane Grey: his cousin; flighty but kind

Mary: his half-sister; stern and unbending

Earl of Hertford: Edward's uncle; encourages and helps Tom in his role as Edward; thinks Edward has lost his memory or gone mad; becomes Duke of Somerset

St. John: court lord; kind and helpful; thinks Edward has lost his memory

Father Andrew: kind old priest; teaches Tom to read and write and the right way of living; killed by John Canty

Miles Hendon: rescues Tom; becomes his friend and protector; dubs himself "Knight of the Kingdom of Dreams and Shadows"

Hugh Hendon: Miles' younger brother; manipulates and deceives to get control of Hendon Hall; tricks Edith into marrying him

Edith Hendon: Miles' cousin with whom he is in love

Blake Andrews: lifelong servant at Hendon Hall; loyal to Miles

The Ruffler: chief of a gang of ruffians

Initiating Activities

Use one or more of the following to introduce the novel.

1. Preview the book by having students note the title, the dedication, the cover illustration, and the teasers on the book cover. Ask them to make individual predictions about the book.

2. Play an audio recording of the music for *The Prince and the Pauper*. This is a piano/vocal demo produced by 2die4Productions and can be located at **www.2die4music.com/prince**.

3. Divide an overhead transparency into two columns. Place the word "prince" as the head of one column and the word "pauper" as head of the other column. Brainstorm with students possible word connotations or definitions for each word and list their responses in the correct column.

4. Place the adage "Clothes make the man" on the overhead transparency. Elicit student response as to the truth of the statement and whether they agree or disagree.

5. Have students respond with "agree" or "disagree" to the following statements.

   - It is easier to adjust to sudden wealth than to sudden poverty.

   - Prestige and/or money make people more sensitive to other's needs.

   - You can go through anything if you have one good friend.

   - We can control our own destiny.

   - Providence (or Fate) controls the destiny of each person.

   - Fantasies rarely evolve into reality.

   - We pay too much attention to a person's outward appearance.

   - A boy always imitates his father's lifestyle.

   - Poor people have no ambition.

   - A child can never overcome a poor environment.

   - A child accepts his/her home life as the normal way to live.

   - Enough money will solve all of our problems.

Character Attribute Web

Directions: Complete the attribute web for a character in *The Prince and the Pauper.*

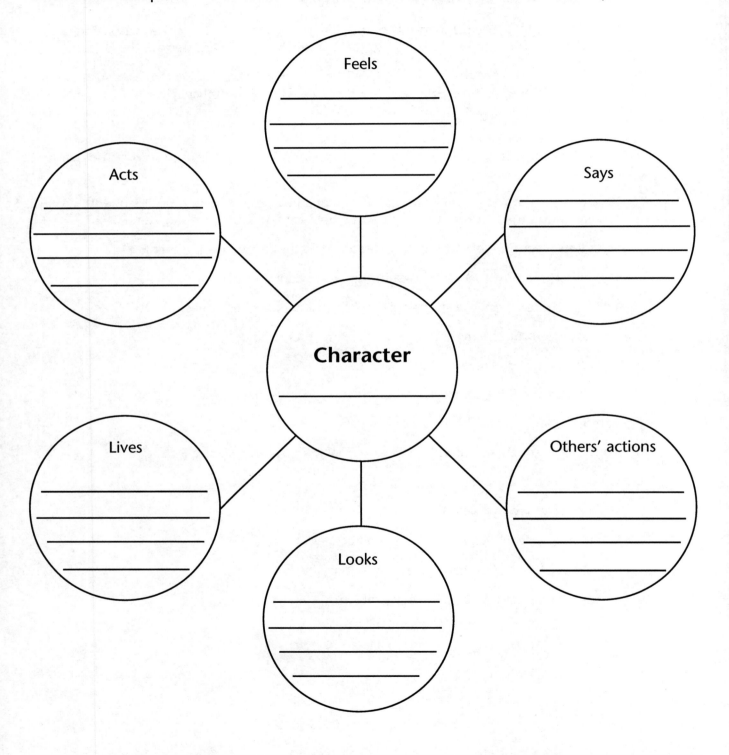

Character Chart

Directions: In the boxes across from each of the feelings, describe an incident or time in the book when each character experienced that feeling. You may use "not applicable" (n/a) if you cannot find an example.

	Tom Canty	Edward Tudor	John Canty	Miles Hendon
Frustration				
Anger				
Fear				
Humiliation				
Relief				

Characters With Character

Directions: A person's **character** is evaluated by his or her actions, statements, and by the way he or she treats others. For each of the attributes listed in the center of the page, write the name of one character from the novel who has that trait, and the name of a character who does **not** have that trait. After each character's name, give an example of an action or statement which proves you have properly evaluated the character.

Has This Trait		Doesn't Have This Trait
	tells the truth	
	keeps promises	
	considers consequences of actions	
	sacrifices for others	
	listens to others without pre-judging them	
	is a good person	
	is kind and caring	

Story Map

Directions: Fill in each box below with information about the novel.

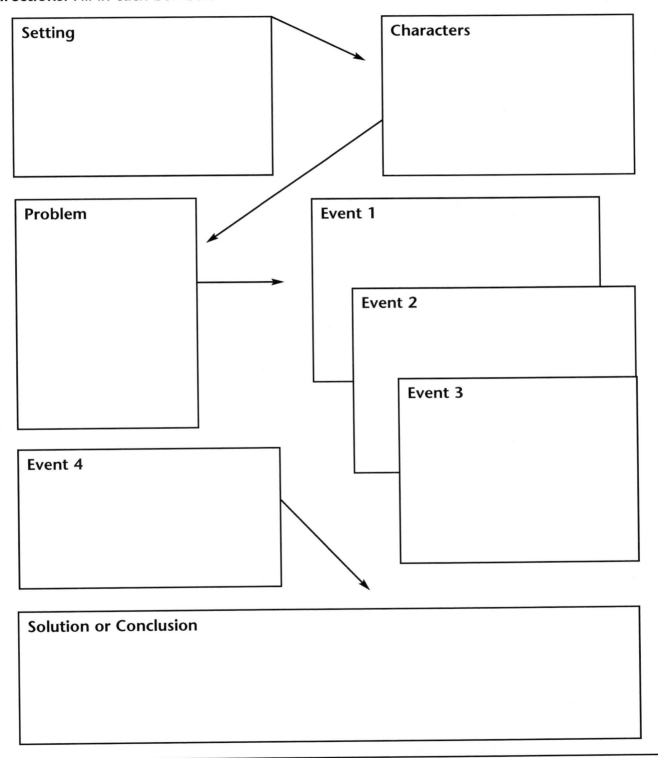

Setting

Characters

Problem

Event 1

Event 2

Event 3

Event 4

Solution or Conclusion

Novel Web Diagram

Directions: Write the book's title in the oval. Then fill in the boxes to summarize the story.

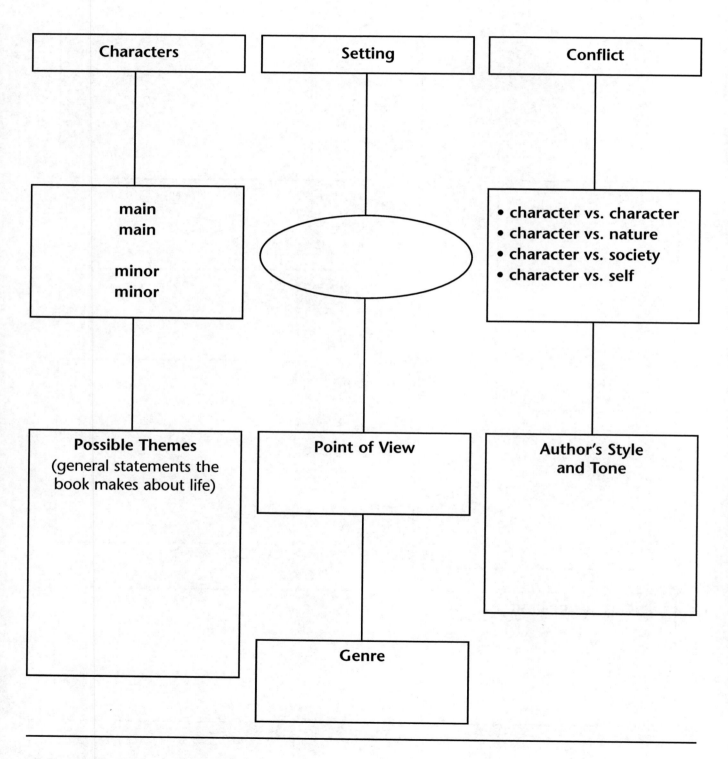

Characters

main
main

minor
minor

Setting

Conflict

- character vs. character
- character vs. nature
- character vs. society
- character vs. self

Possible Themes
(general statements the book makes about life)

Point of View

Author's Style and Tone

Genre

Cause-Effect

Directions: To plot cause and effect in a story, first list the sequence of events. Then mark causes with a C and effects with an E. Sometimes in a chain of events, one item may be both a cause and an effect. Draw arrows from cause statements to the appropriate effects.

Events in the story:

1.

2.

3.

4.

5.

6.

7.

8.

9.

10.

Another way to map cause and effect is to look for an effect and then backtrack to the single or multiple causes.

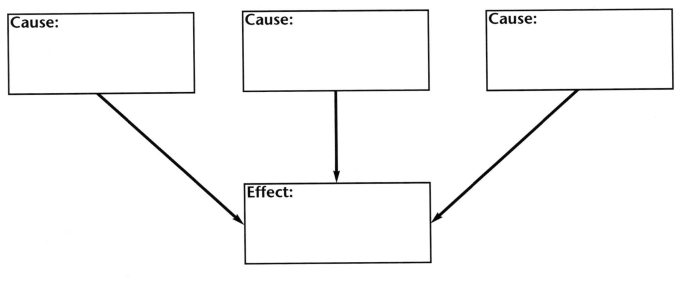

Chapters 1–3, pp. 1-15

Tom Canty, a young beggar, and Edward Tudor, Prince of Wales, meet accidentally, exchange clothes, and switch their identities.

Vocabulary

paupers (2)	offal (3)	rabble (4)	mendicancy (5)
melancholy (7)	obeisance (7)	mien (12)	raiment (12)
cudgel (13)			

Discussion Questions

1. Contrast the births of Tom Canty and Edward Tudor. Note their respective homes. *(Tom, born to the impoverished Canty family, was not wanted at his birth. Edward Tudor, born the same day to King Henry VIII and Jane Seymour, was welcomed by his parents and all England. At birth, Tom was wrapped in rags; Edward was wrapped in silks and satins. Tom lives a meager life in a despicable neighborhood called Offal Court. Edward lives a pampered, luxurious life in the king's palace. pp. 1-3, 9-12)*

2. Examine Tom's relationship and interaction with the following: John Canty and his mother, Tom's mother, Nan and Bet, and Father Andrew. *(Tom's father, John Canty, is a thief, and John's mother is a beggar. They both get drunk, fight, curse, and beat Tom regularly and severely, especially if he comes home empty-handed from his efforts at begging. Nan and Bet are Tom's fifteen-year-old twin sisters. Although Tom, his mother, and his sisters are not like John and his mother, the children are forced to beg. Tom's mother loves him, consoles him after a beating, and slips him her own scraps of food. The Canty family is dirty and unkempt. Father Andrew is a poor old priest who teaches Tom to read and write and tries to teach all the children the right way to live. pp. 3-5)*

3. Discuss how Tom views his life. *(He is not unhappy because he has never known anything different. He begs just enough to save himself from the beatings. He loves to listen to Father Andrew's tales and legends, especially those about kings. He reads the priest's books and enjoys playing in the Thames River and watching events around London. pp. 4-6)*

4. Discuss Tom's recurrent dream and its effect on him. *(He dreams about living the life of a prince in a regal palace. His dream world causes him to lament his shabby clothing and dirty body. He begins to act like a prince, and his speech and actions become princely. The other children in his neighborhood begin to view him with awe and to consider him wise and gifted. He organizes a "royal court" and daily enacts ceremonies of a real court. One desire that haunts him day and night is to see a real prince. pp. 5-7)*

5. Examine the initial meeting between Tom and Edward. Contrast their appearance and note their individual "titles" on page 10. *(As he wanders around London, Tom comes to the gate of the castle at Westminster. Tom, hungry, frail, and dressed in rags, sees Edward, strong, healthy, and dressed in silks and satins, through the bars of the gate. As Tom tries to get close to the gate to see the prince, the guards grab him roughly and order him to mind his manners. Edward commands the guards to open the gates and let Tom in; Tom: the Prince of Poverty; Edward: the Prince of Limitless Plenty. pp. 8-11)*

6. Discuss what Tom and Edward reveal to each other. *(Tom tells Edward about his mistreatment at the hands of his father and his grandmother. Edward tells Tom that his father can be angry and strike others, but he spares Edward physical blows, sometimes lashing him with his tongue. Tom reveals that his mother and his twin sisters are good and never bring him pain. Edward reveals that his sister, Elizabeth, and his cousin, Jane Grey, are happy and gracious, but that his sister Mary is gloomy and won't let her servants smile. Edward learns that Tom has no servants and his family has only one garment each. Tom tells Edward that Father Andrew teaches him. pp. 9-12)*

7. Discuss the circumstances that lead to the reversal of the roles of Tom and Edward. Elicit student response as to the plausibility of this happening. *(Tom tells Edward about life in Offal Court. He makes the entertainment, e.g., Punch and Judy shows, the boys' fights, and wading and swimming in the canals and river sound so enticing that Edward expresses the desire to enjoy Tom's life just once. Tom expresses his desire to be clothed like a prince just once. The boys decide to exchange clothes. Looking at themselves in the mirror, they discover they look and speak exactly alike. Edward notices a bruise on Tom's hand and rushes out the palace gates to reprimand the guard. Thinking it is Tom, the guard hustles him away. The crowd follows him. pp. 13-15)*

8. **Prediction:** What will happen to Tom? to Edward?

Supplementary Activities

1. Have students begin individual bio-poems for Tom and Edward. Add to these as more facts emerge. Pattern—Line 1: Name; Line 2: Lives (place)...; Line 3: Four descriptive words; Line 4: Relationships, i.e., Son of, Brother of, Friend of...; Line 5: Likes to...; Line 6: Feels...; Line 7: Needs...; Line 8: Gives...; Line 9: Fears...; Line 10: Would like to...; Line 11: Becomes...

2. Note the literary devices: **Metaphor**—man-at-arms: living statue (p. 9) **Simile**—They stopped stock-still where they were, like...statues (p. 10).

Chapters 4–6, pp. 16-35

Edward and Tom begin life under their assumed identities. Each tries unsuccessfully to convince other people that there has been a mix-up.

Vocabulary

prodigious (16)	plebeian (18)	patrician (20)	menial (21)
palter (29)	distemper (31)	stripling (32)	

Discussion Questions

1. Discuss Edward's first night as "Tom" and why no one will believe his true identity. *(He finally escapes the crowd but realizes he doesn't know where he is. He recognizes Christ's Church, a refuge for poor, forsaken children, and believes he can find help there. When he announces that he is the Prince of Wales, the boys ridicule and mock him because, although he speaks like a prince, he is dressed like a beggar. The boys begin to hit him and call the dogs to chase him. Bruised, bleeding, and muddy, he searches for and finally finds Offal Court. John Canty grabs Edward and thinks he's gone crazy when he announces that he is the Prince of Wales. He drags the boy home, promising a beating when they get there. pp. 16-19)*

2. Discuss Edward's resolution after his mistreatment by the boys at Christ's Church. Have students refer to note 2 at the end of the book. *(He vows that when he is king, the boys will not only have food and shelter but that they will also have teachers so they can learn from books the things they need to fill their minds and hearts. Note 2: Christ's Hospital was originally founded to shelter, feed, and clothe children from the streets, not as a school. pp. 18, 223)*

3. Discuss Tom's first experience as "Edward." *(When Edward doesn't return, Tom becomes afraid that someone will catch him in the prince's clothes. He thinks the servants are mocking him when they bow to him. He kneels before Jane Gray and tries to convince her of his true identity, but she runs away in fear. The servants decide he has gone mad or lost his memory but resolve to tell no one. He is escorted to Edward's father, King Henry VIII, who also fails to detect that this is not Edward. pp. 19-22)*

4. Examine Tom's meeting with Henry VIII. Discuss why the king doesn't believe Tom's tale and how he diagnoses Tom's "ailment." *(The king speaks gently to Tom and assures him of his love. Tom reacts in fear, which leads the king to conclude that his son is not well. Tom tries to convince the king that he is not Edward, and the king devises a test to prove his child's identity. He asks Tom a question in Latin; Tom responds. When the king asks him a question in French, Tom cannot respond, and the king declares that his son is mad, but it is not permanent. He rationalizes that "Edward's" malady comes from too much study and confinement. He orders them to do away with books and teachers and to encourage Edward in sports until he becomes healthy again. Anyone who spreads a tale about Edward's madness will be hanged. pp. 22-26)*

5. Discuss the help Tom receives as he adapts to Edward's life. *(The Earl of Hertford and Lord St. John become Tom's guardians. They guide him to give the right responses to questions. Princess Elizabeth comforts him and tells him his problems are the result of his ailment. She acts as a buffer between Tom and Jane. pp. 28-32)*

6. Analyze the Earl of Hertford and Lord St. John's assessment of Tom and their conclusions. *(They are afraid "Edward" has gone mad. St. John speaks of differences in "Edward" and wonders if he really is the prince. The Earl declares that St. John must never voice this treason and assures him this is the true prince because there couldn't possibly be two identical boys in the kingdom. pp. 33-35)*

Supplementary Activities

1. Note John Canty's statement that Tom is as mad as any at Bedlam. Have students research Bedlam and participate in an oral discussion of treatment for the mentally ill in 16th century England.

2. Have students sketch a portrayal of the metaphor, "The castle was a gilded cage" (p. 26).

3. Literary devices: **Metaphors**—houses in Offal Court: swarming hives of poverty and misery (p. 19); people in the streets: human vermin (p. 19) **Simile**—servants and pages clothed like butterflies (p. 21)

Chapters 7–9, pp. 36-46

Tom learns to conduct himself like a prince. Even though Tom tries to reveal his true identity, King Henry VIII and members of the court believe he is Edward.

Vocabulary

vagaries (37)   eccentricity (38)   panoply (39)   halberdiers (43)

Discussion Questions

1. Discuss Tom's servants and his reaction to them. Note the humor of Tom's need to scratch his nose. *(The servants are there to do everything for him from placing the napkin around his neck to tasting his food before he eats it. He has 384 servants. Because of their close attention, Tom is afraid to scratch his own nose. This presents a dilemma for the servants because there is no "Hereditary Scratcher." All are relieved when Tom scratches his own nose. pp. 35-38)*

2. Discuss King Henry VIII's dilemma about the Great Seal. *(He has ordered the execution of the Duke of Norfolk and needs the Seal to confirm Duke's doom. He can't find it and is reminded that he gave it to Edward. Tom doesn't know what it is or where it might be. The king decides he can use the small Seal. pp. 40-42)*

3. Examine the changes in Tom's life during his first twenty-four hours as Edward. *(He dresses splendidly, is surrounded by servants, and dines on wonderful food. Because of his manner of speech and conduct, he is accepted as the prince and quickly adapts to his new role. pp. 36-46)*

4. **Prediction:** Will Tom be able to convince the court nobles that he is not Edward? If so, how?

Supplementary Activities

1. Have students write a cinquain poem about royalty. Pattern—Line 1: the title, one word (noun); Line 2: two words to describe the title; Line 3: three words to express action concerning the title; Line 4: four words to express feeling(s) about the title; Line 5: one word that is a synonym for the title.

2. Literary devices: **Metaphors**—Tom: target; Jane's Greek phrases: shaft; problems: snags and sandbars (p. 31); two lords: guardian angels; Tom's guidance in conversation: dangerous channel (p. 32) **Anachronism**—use a dog or a plumber (p. 37)

Chapters 10–11, pp. 47-61

Edward is mocked and severely beaten when he tries to convince John Canty that he is not Tom. After Edward escapes from Canty, Miles Hendon rescues him.

Vocabulary

mummeries (48)   wenches (49)   commiseration (50)   canker (54)
usurper (55)   limpid (56)   rapier (59)

Discussion Questions

1. Discuss the Cantys' reaction to Edward's attempts to identify himself. Note Tom's mother's test of his identity. *(When Edward announces his true identity, Tom's mother and sisters run to him with sympathy. John Canty makes Nan and Bet kneel before Edward in mockery. The girls plead for their brother. Canty demands money from "Tom's" night of begging, then he and Tom's grandmother severely beat him. The twins and their mother comfort Tom. The test is based on Tom's reaction to suddenly being startled. He always puts his hand before his eyes with the palm inward. Mrs. Canty flashes a light in his face but Edward does not respond as Tom would have. She will not accept the results of the test because she can't give up her boy. pp. 47-52)*

2. Discuss the one person who tries to defend "Tom" against his father and the mob, and the results of this defense. *(Father Andrew tries to keep Canty from striking "Tom" on the head with a cudgel. Canty then strikes Father Andrew on his head. Father Andrew dies and the Cantys must leave the neighborhood. Edward manages to escape as they are fleeing. pp. 53-55)*

3. Analyze Edward's reaction to his vision of Tom playing the role of prince and what this reveals about Edward. *(He decides that he will allow Tom reasonable time for spiritual preparation and then have him hanged, drawn, and quartered for high treason. Edward does not understand that Tom is also in a dilemma and believes Tom is just enjoying himself and taking advantage of his situation. Edward forgets that it was he who insisted they change clothes, and he seeks revenge. p. 55)*

4. Contrast Tom and Edward's experiences at Guildhall. Examine the changes that occur in the life of each boy. *(Tom, Elizabeth, and Jane are greeted with great ceremony and seated under a rich canopy, with servants standing behind them. They enjoy a great banquet and wonderful performances. Before leaving Guildhall, news comes of Henry VIII's death, and Tom becomes king of England. Edward, ragged and hungry, stands outside the gates proclaiming his true identity and his rights. He is mocked by the crowd but is determined to stand his ground. Miles Hendon defends Edward and rescues him from the mob. pp. 58-61)*

5. Analyze Tom's first official act after being declared king and what this reveals about him. *(He revokes Henry VIII's order for the execution of the Duke of Norfolk. This reveals his compassion and causes the people to proclaim that the reign of blood is ended. pp. 60-61)*

6. **Prediction:** Will Tom now use his power to find Edward and restore him to his rightful place?

Supplementary Activities

1. Have students draw a caricature depicting the metaphor, "John Canty and his mother are swine" (p. 49).

2. Literary devices: **Metaphor**—crowds at London Bridge: swarming hive of humanity, tossing sea of life (pp. 54-55) **Simile**—They (fireworks) seemed like jeweled lances thrust aloft (p. 56).

Chapters 12–13, pp. 62-78

Miles Hendon takes Edward to his room at the inn and encounters Edward's traits of royalty. Edward is lured away from the inn.

Vocabulary

waif (62)   inane (64)   soliloquizing (66)   insolent (67)
alacrity (67)   suborned (70)

Discussion Questions

1. Analyze the effect on Edward when he hears of his father's death. *(The news sends a chill to his heart and a shudder through his body. He begins to cry with bitter grief and remembers the kindness and gentleness of the man whom most people viewed with terror. He feels forlorn, outcast, and forsaken. The cry, "Long live King Edward the Sixth" thrills him with pride because he realizes he is now the king. p. 62)*

2. Discuss Miles Hendon's interaction with Edward. Note Miles' request in response to Edward's offer to grant his desire. *(Miles leads Edward away from the crowd. John Canty attempts to recapture Edward, but Miles threatens to kill Canty unless he leaves. Miles takes Edward to his room at the inn, where Edward demands his royal rights, e.g., takes Miles' bed, tells him to prepare his food, wash him, and stand in his presence. Miles, thinking Edward's mind is disordered, complies with Edward's demands and vows to himself that he will cure Edward. Miles asks that the "king" grant him and his heirs forever the right to sit in his presence. Edward grants the request. pp. 62-73)*

3. Examine what Miles reveals about himself. *(He has been away from his home for ten years. His mother is dead. His father, Sir Richard Hendon, is a baronet and master of Hendon Hall. He has two brothers: Arthur the elder and Hugh the younger. Sir Richard and Arthur are kind-hearted and generous, but Hugh is mean-spirited and treacherous. Hugh has always been his father's favorite. Miles had loved his cousin Edith, who was betrothed to Arthur. Hugh also wanted her and deceived their father into believing that Miles had committed a crime. His father sent Miles to war and, after three years, he was captured and imprisoned for seven years. He has just arrived back in England and plans to return to Hendon Hall, not knowing what has happened there during his absence. pp. 68-70)*

4. Analyze the irony of Miles' resolve to cure Edward of his madness and help him "make himself a name." *(Edward is not mad and needs no cure. He already has a "name for himself," Edward VI, King of England. p. 70)*

5. Examine the circumstances surrounding Edward's disappearance and what this reveals about him. *(Miles leaves Edward asleep in the room at the inn. When he returns after purchasing some clothes for Edward, he finds the child gone. He discovers from the innkeeper that a boy had come to tell Edward that Miles had sent for him. Miles realizes the boy who came after Edward has deceived him by arranging the covers to make it appear that Edward was asleep. The innkeeper recalls seeing a ruffian join the two boys near the bridge. Miles realizes that Edward went with the boy because of his loyalty to Miles. pp. 74-78)*

6. **Prediction:** Will Miles find Edward?

Supplementary Activities

1. Have students write a brief response to Miles' self-appointed title, "Knight of the Kingdom of Dreams and Shadows." This can be a paragraph or a short poem beginning, "I am the Knight of the Kingdom of Dreams and Shadows."

2. Have students draw a caricature of Hugh Hendon based on the metaphor, "Hugh is a reptile" (p. 69).

Chapters 14–16, pp. 79-106

Tom begins his reign as King Edward VI. He reveals insight and compassion as he deals with various situations.

Vocabulary

obsequies (83)   preamble (83)   ducal (84)   formidable (97)
veneration (103)

Discussion Questions

1. Discuss Tom's first day as King of England and its effect on him. *(He awakens from a dream in which he is back in his own home. He realizes he is still a captive and a king. He goes through the lengthy process of being dressed and prepared for the day. Everyone treats him with great respect. Under the Earl of Hertford's guidance, Tom conducts himself with dignity and does as he is told, signing orders and greeting foreign dignitaries. pp. 79-85)*

2. Discuss Tom's solution to the king's household financial difficulties, the response to his suggestion, and what this reveals about him. *(Tom gasps at the enormity of the vast household expenses. He discovers that a large part of the debts have not been paid, the king's coffers are nearly empty, and the servants have not been paid. Tom proclaims they are going to the dogs and suggests that they move to a smaller house. Hertford stops Tom with pressure on his arm and continues to keep Tom from making mistakes. Tom's reaction reveals his common sense. pp. 83-85)*

3. Examine the role and importance of a whipping boy to Edward and his importance to Tom. *(He receives the whippings Edward deserves for not doing his school work or for other misbehavior. The whipping boy, thinking he is helping with Edward's cure, fills in much of the background information of Edward's life. Tom gains valuable information about Edward's childhood and people and about matters relating to the court. pp. 85-90)*

4. Examine Humphrey Marlow's request of Tom and Tom's response. Analyze the irony of his role as whipping boy. *(Even though Tom is now king, Humphrey asks him not to turn him away as whipping boy. Tom vows that his role will be permanent, then dubs him "Hereditary Grand Whipping Boy to the royal house of England." Irony: Humphrey suffers unjust whippings because of Edward, yet if he loses his "job," he and his family will have no income. He calls his back his bread, and if his back is idle, he will starve. pp. 88-89)*

5. Discuss the impending execution of the man, woman, and young girl and what this reveals about England's laws and modes of punishment. Analyze Tom's reaction and what this reveals

about him. *(Tom observes the three being led to their execution. He commands that they be brought to him. He learns that the man is going to be boiled alive for allegedly killing someone with poison. The woman and the girl are going to be hanged for allegedly selling themselves to the devil and then using this power to bring a destructive storm to the area. They supposedly accomplished this by pulling off their stockings. After questioning the prisoners, Tom discovers how flimsy the evidence is against them. He sets the man free because of his personal observation of the man pulling a drowning boy from the water at the time the alleged crime took place. He proves the woman and girl's innocence by commanding them to pull their stockings off and produce a storm. They are unable to cause a storm. Tom sets all three prisoners free. He exerts his authority by forbidding further executions by boiling the prisoner in oil. His actions demonstrate his discernment and compassion. pp. 93-102)*

6. Examine the response of the court officials to Tom's dealings with the prisoners. *(When Tom ends the practice of boiling prisoners in oil, the Earl of Hertford shows profound gratification. When he sets the condemned prisoners free, the court responds with admiration and applause for Tom's intelligence and spirit. They recognize Tom's wisdom and believe that he shows the strength a king needs. pp. 96-102)*

Supplementary Activities
1. Read aloud Judith Viorst's poem, "If I Were in Charge of the World." Have students write a short poem beginning with the same phrase. Reference: Judith Viorst, *If I Were in Charge of the World* (New York: Aladdin Books, Macmillan, 1981) 2-3.

2. Divide the class into two groups, one group to stage a mock trial for the man accused of poisoning a man, the other group to stage a mock trial for the woman and the girl.

Chapters 17–18, pp. 107-126
John Canty recaptures Edward and takes him to a gang of ruffians. Edward is forced to participate in the gang's activities, but he is finally able to escape.

Vocabulary
rue (108)	truculent (110)	blasphemy (113)	ironical (116)
epithets (119)	Providence (121)	uncanny (122)	pungent (123)
kine (126)			

Discussion Questions
1. Discuss what happens to Edward after he leaves Miles' room at the inn. *(He continues to follow the boy, Hugo, because Hugo tells him Miles is wounded and needs him. John Canty recaptures Edward but believes he is mad when Edward again says he is the king. Canty changes their names to John Hobbs and his son, Jack. He takes Edward to a gang of ruffians in which he had formerly participated. The gang is made up of some criminals and some innocent victims of King Henry VIII's laws, e.g., farmers who lost their land. pp. 107-114)*

2. Examine life in the gang, the role of the Ruffler, and Edward's reactions to the gang. Analyze what the gang members reveal about the plight of the poor in England and its effect on

Edward. *(The gang is comprised of both sexes of varied ages and sizes. The women are all loud, foul-mouthed, and dirty. They all live together in a barn and have nightly orgies. Through their conversation, Edward learns background information about the gang. It is comprised of murderers, thieves, fugitives, and newcomers such as farmers who have been driven from their land, forced to beg, and eventually branded as slaves. The Ruffler is the chief and controls the group. Edward's reaction: announces his identity as Edward, king of England and vows that the escaped "slave" will not be hanged. Edward tells John Canty that he will have him hanged as a murderer. The Ruffler saves Edward from Canty's wrath by knocking him down and calling for the gang members to proclaim "Long live Edward, king of England!" The gang mocks Edward by crowning, robing, and enthroning him, then kneeling before him and calling him "Foo-foo the First, king of the Mooncalves." Edward is heartbroken because of their reaction to his offer of kindness. pp. 110-117)*

3. Discuss Edward's role as a member of the gang and his escape. *(Hugo is placed in charge of Edward. At their first "assignment," he tells Edward they will beg since he sees nothing worth stealing. When Edward refuses to beg, Hugo tells him that he must act as decoy, then proceeds with his plan to trick a man into giving them money. Hugo runs away after Edward tells the man that Hugo is a beggar and a thief, and Edward escapes. At night he takes refuge in a barn, where he sleeps next to a calf. pp. 118-126)*

4. **Prediction:** Will Edward ever be able to return to his rightful place as king?

Supplementary Activities

1. Have students write a cinquain poem about the gang.

2. Have students write a metaphor or simile poem reflecting Edward's happiness the night in the barn (p. 125). Pattern—Line 1: noun (title); Lines 2-4: something about the subject (Each line should describe the subject in a different way); Line 5: a metaphor that begins with the noun from line 1 or a simile that begins with the noun from line 1 and includes "like" or "as."

3. Literary devices: **Metaphor**—night wind: music (p. 125) **Simile**—rustling of dry leaves like human whispers (p. 122)

Chapters 19–22, pp. 127-151

Edward's adventures include time with the peasants and a near-death experience with a crazy hermit. Miles again rescues him.

Vocabulary

comely (127)	sagacity (130)	magnanimous (131)	judiciously (134)
patriarchs (136)	archangel (136)	impotent (141)	complaisance (142)
copse (143)	mortification (147)	infamous (149)	

Discussion Questions

1. Examine Edward's experience with the peasants. Contrast the children's reception of him with their mother's. *(After Edward spends the night in the barn, two little girls discover him. With childhood trust, they believe he is the king. He resolves that, when he has his rightful place as king, he will always honor little children. Their mother treats him kindly but believes he is crazy.*

She searches for something he can do well but finds him unknowledgeable and inept in everything except matters of the court. He leaves the peasants' home when he hears Hugo and Canty approaching. pp. 127-132)

2. Analyze the irony of the meal Edward shares with the peasant family. *(Both the peasants and Edward waive the customs of "rank." The woman allows Edward to eat with his "betters," i.e., the family, rather than feed him in the corner like a tramp or a dog. Edward humbles himself to the level of the peasants instead of requiring the woman and children to stand and wait on him while he eats alone. Neither the peasants nor Edward is aware that they have breached the rules of protocol. p. 131)*

3. Discuss Edward's experience with the hermit and why the hermit becomes vindictive. *(Edward is relieved to find a true holy man but begins to think he is the prisoner of a madman. The hermit believes he is an archangel who has shaken hands with some of the Old Testament patriarchs and has seen God face to face. He is convinced he was chosen to be the pope but blames the king for robbing him of his identity by dissolving his religious order and leaving the monks homeless. When Edward tells the hermit that King Henry is dead and that he, Edward, is the king's son, the hermit plans his retaliation against the king. While Edward sleeps, the hermit sharpens a rusty old knife and ties up the boy. When Edward awakens, the hermit commands the terrified boy to pray the prayer for the dying. They hear Edward's voice, but the hermit tricks Miles into leaving without Edward. Canty and Hugo enter the cabin and free Edward, taking him back to the gang. pp. 133-144)*

4. Discuss Miles' search for and rescue of Edward. Elicit student response as to why the hermit so easily tricks Miles. *(He tracks Edward to the hermit's cabin, hears Edward's moans, but is distracted by the hermit's explanation that he hears the wind and that Edward has gone on an errand for the "archangel." After being returned to the gang, Hugo tricks Edward into being caught with a stolen pig. During the uproar that follows, Miles comes to Edward's aid; Student responses will vary. Suggestion: Twain uses Miles' gullibility toward the hermit to show the reverence with which "holy men" were viewed. pp. 145-151)*

5. **Prediction:** What will happen to Edward and Miles?

Supplementary Activities

1. Have students prepare an acrostic for the word "treachery."

2. Have students draw a caricature based on the metaphor comparing the hermit to a spider and Edward to an insect (p. 140).

3. Have students write a brief explanation of the metaphor that calls Edward the "Seed of the Church's spoiler" (p. 141).

23

Chapters 23–26, pp. 152-172

Edward and Miles are reunited. Miles' anticipated return to Hendon Hall ends in rejection and imprisonment.

Vocabulary

consternation (154)   decorum (154)   flogging (155)   undulation (161)
leal (165)   imperviously (169)   miscreant (171)

Discussion Questions

1. Discuss Edward and Miles' reunion. Analyze what this reveals about both of them. *(After Miles finds Edward, he accompanies the boy to the judge. Miles, playing on the boy's assumed royalty, encourages Edward to abide by the laws and submit to the court's authority as he would expect one of his subjects to do. Edward follows Miles' instructions. Their interactions reveal their mutual admiration, friendship, and trust. pp. 150-153)*

2. Discuss the incident involving the stolen pig and examine Miles' ingenuity. *(The lady from whom the pig was stolen gives its worth as three shillings and an eightpence. The penalty for stealing anything worth more than 13 pence is death by hanging. When the woman realizes Edward will hang for the crime, she reduces the pig's worth to an eightpence, and Edward is sentenced to a short time in jail and a public flogging. The constable takes advantage of the woman's oath and, under threat of disclosing her "crime" of false testimony about the pig's worth, buys the pig for eightpence. Miles' ingenuity: threatens to tell the judge what the constable has done and demands that the constable give the pig back to the woman and allow Edward to escape. pp. 153-159)*

3. Contrast Miles Hendon's anticipation of his return to Hendon Hall and the reality of the return. Discuss how he is received, what he learns, and his resolve. *(Anticipation: He is excited and expects a joyful welcome with his family being delighted and thankful for his return. Reality: Hugh denies knowing him and tells him the family received a letter telling of Miles' death. Edith also denies his identity. He discovers that his father and elder brother Arthur are both dead, all of the loyal servants are gone, and Edith is Hugh's wife. He resolves that he is the master of Hendon Hall and will remain so. pp. 160-167)*

4. Analyze Edith's reaction to Miles and her warning. Elicit student response concerning the reasons for Edith's denial. *(Edith comes to Miles and, although she continues to deny his identity, she warns him that Hugh is master of the region and will tell others that Miles is a mad imposter, that no one will defend him, and that he will be punished. She tells him that Hugh is a tyrant and she is his slave. She begs Miles to leave and offers him money. pp. 165-167, 170-172)*

5. **Prediction:** What will happen to Miles and Edward after they are taken to prison?

Supplementary Activities

1. Have students write a letter from Edward to his uncle, the Earl of Hertford, in which he explains his true identity (see pages 168-169).

2. Have students write name poems for Hugh Hendon and Edith.

Chapters 27–29, pp. 173-189

Miles Hendon and Edward are imprisoned, where Edward learns of injustices in his "kingdom." Hendon learns the truth about Hugh from an old servant.

Vocabulary

taciturn (173)	seditious (176)	vagabond (183)	pillory (183)
sardonic (185)	fortitude (185)	evanescent (188)	

Discussion Questions

1. Discuss Miles and Edward's imprisonment. Examine Blake Andrews' role. *(After being taken prisoners at Hendon Hall, the two are imprisoned and chained for a week in a large room at a dirty, crowded prison. Andrews, a servant of the Hendons all his life, comes to the prison and pretends to denounce Miles as an imposter. After the jailer leaves, Andrews whispers to Miles that he does know him and will proclaim the truth if Miles tells him to, even though Andrews will die for it. Andrews comes often on the pretense of "abusing" Miles. He gives Miles the following information: Arthur died six years before; the family received a letter telling of Miles' death; Sir Richard, on his deathbed, insisted that Edith marry Hugh; Hugh is cruel to Edith and the servants; Edith discovered that Hugh had written the letter about Miles' death. pp. 173-176)*

2. Examine the news Andrews brings Miles and Edward about the English court. *(News of the kingdom: there is a rumor that the young king is mad; King Henry will be buried in a day or two and the new king will be crowned; Hugh is going to the coronation; the Earl of Hertford is now the Duke of Somerset, Lord Protector; the young King Edward is highly respected. This news depresses Edward as he wonders if the urchin Tom can possibly be posing as the king. He feels an urgency to get to London. pp. 176-178)*

3. Examine the "crimes" of the two women who are chained near Edward, their punishment, Edward's reaction to their plight, and his resolve. *(They are Baptists. The women avoid telling Edward what their punishment will be. The next morning the women are gone, and Edward thinks they have been released. The prisoners are led out to watch proceedings in the courtyard, and Edward sees the women chained to posts. He thinks they are going to be beaten but realizes they will be burned to death. Edward vows he will never forget the scene. As he learns from other prisoners how unjust their punishment is for trivial crimes, he vows that he will set the prisoners free and that he will sweep the unjust laws from the statute books. pp. 178-181)*

4. Discuss Miles' punishment and Edward's reaction. *(He must sit in the stocks for two hours for pretending to be Miles Hendon and assaulting Hugh. Edward's reaction: confronts officers and says he is the king. Edward is seized. Miles begs them to let Edward go and says he will take the boy's lashes. Edward weeps and resolves he will never forget Miles' loyal deed nor will he forget those who perpetrate the punishment. Because Miles has saved Edward from shame, he dubs him "Earl." Miles' stoic acceptance of his punishment earns the respect of the mob. pp. 183-186)*

5. Discuss Miles' decision and the results. *(He resolves to go to London and beg the king for justice. He remembers his father's friend, Sir Humphrey Marlow, and hopes he can help him. He and Edward go to London but are separated in the throng of people who have gathered for Coronation Day. pp. 187-189)*

6. **Prediction:** What will happen to Edward in London? to Miles?

25

Supplementary Activities

1. Have students write a rhyme about Miles' and Edward's experiences on London Bridge, to be set to the tune of the children's song, "London Bridge."

2. Note the metaphor, "the fog of humiliation and depression which had settled down upon his (Miles') spirits lifted and blew away" (p. 188).

Chapters 30–32, pp. 190-212

Tom enjoys the luxuries of a king while Edward wanders around ragged and forlorn. London prepares for Edward VI's coronation. Just before Tom is crowned king, Edward appears, proclaims that he is king, and, with Tom's help, proves his true identity.

Vocabulary

salaaming (191)	penury (192)	vassals (192)	rent (193)
largess (195)	effigy (196)	eulogistic (196)	transept (201)
apparition (203)	fealty (204)	dynasty (205)	

Discussion Questions

1. Contrast the lives of Edward, the wanderer, and Tom, the king. *(Edward wanders around the land, poorly dressed and fed, mistreated by tramps, imprisoned with thieves and murderers, called an idiot and an imposter. He is wedged in the crowd, dirty, ragged, and tired, as he watches preparations for the coronation. Tom is splendidly dressed and has tripled the number of his servants. He loves the life of royalty and enjoys being pampered and ordering others to do as he wishes. The night before the coronation, he sleeps in a rich bed, guarded by loyal men. pp. 190-191)*

2. Examine Tom in his role as king and his thoughts of his former life. Apply the adage, "Out of sight, out of mind" to Tom. *(He has lost his fears and misgivings and has become confident in his role as king. He is kind and gentle, champions the oppressed, and battles unjust laws. At times he turns his anger toward the nobles. He asks God to change Mary's heart. At first he remembers and is concerned about Edward, and his thoughts of him make Tom feel guilty and ashamed. Gradually, however, he ceases to think of Edward. At first Tom grieves for his mother and sisters, yet he shudders at the thought of their coming into court, dirty and clothed in rags. He finally almost forgets them but feels despicable when they do come to his mind. pp. 191-192)*

3. Discuss Tom's reaction when he recognizes friends from Offal Court and his mother during the coronation procession. Analyze what this reveals about Tom. *(He wishes his friends could recognize him now as a real king but realizes he can't acknowledge them because it would cost him too much. He is shocked when he sees his mother and she recognizes him by his childhood habit of throwing his hands before his eyes. When she runs to him, hugs his leg, and cries, "O my child, my darling!" Tom replies, "I do not know you, woman." He immediately feels ashamed and bows his head, but does not return to her. This experience destroys all of his joy at being crowned king. When he finally proclaims that the woman is his mother, the duke thinks he's gone mad again. pp. 195-199)*

4. Examine the turn of events at the coronation. *(As the Archbishop of Canterbury lifts the crown over Tom's head, Edward appears, bareheaded and clothed in rags. Edward forbids the crowning of Tom and declares that he is the true king. Several men grab Edward, but Tom proclaims the truth. Panic ensues, the Lord Protector thinks the king has gone mad again, and tells the guards to seize Edward. Tom stamps his foot, cries out that Edward is the king, runs to Edward and falls on his knees, swearing his loyalty to the real king. The Lord Protector recognizes Edward and begins to quiz him about the location of the Great Seal, knowing this will prove his true identity. When the seal is not found in the place Edward reveals, Tom guides him through the steps to locate the seal. The seal is recovered, and Edward is crowned king. pp. 203-211)*

5. Analyze why Lord St. John makes obeisance to both Edward and Tom and note the insecurity of the crowd around the two boys. *(St. John is unsure who is the real king and wants to be "right," so he bows at a neutral point halfway between the two. When it seems that Edward is the king, the crowd gradually leaves Tom standing alone to gather around Edward. After St. John announces his inability to find the Great Seal, the crowd gravitates back toward Tom. pp. 206-207)*

6. Examine Tom's final moment as king and Edward's first moment as king. *(St. John brings the Great Seal, and the crowd raises a shout for the true king. Tom asks Edward to take the royal garments and return the ragged garments to him. The Lord Protector wants Tom stripped and flung into the Tower, but Edward assures the Lord Protector that Tom will not be punished. He reminds the Lord Protector of his precarious position since Tom was the one who gave him the title. Tom's revelation that he has been cracking nuts with the Great Seal confirms beyond any doubt that Edward is the true king. pp. 210-211)*

Supplementary Activities

1. Have students design a Great Seal that depicts their individual characteristics.

2. Have students write a eulogistic rhyme that explains the splendor of coronation day (see page 196).

3. Guide students to find and understand the following similes: gangs of workmen as busy as ants (p. 192); White Tower stood out...as a mountain peak projects above a cloud rack (p. 193); (Tom's) grandeurs...seemed to fall away like rotten rags (p. 197); pageant went winding like a radiant and interminable serpent (p. 197); words smote upon the king's soul as the strokes of a funeral bell (p. 198); peeress clothed like Solomon (p. 201); movement such as is observed in a kaleidoscope (p. 207).

Chapter 33–Conclusion, pp. 212-222

Miles and Edward are reunited. The denouement reveals the destiny of each of the primary characters.

Vocabulary

musings (213)   torpid (218)   benignant (222)

Discussion Questions

1. Discuss Miles and Edward's reunion. Note the unusual circumstances. *(Edward sends his whipping boy to search for Miles. He, not knowing the boy's identity, asks him if he knows Sir Humphrey Marlow, then discovers the boy is Marlow's son. The whipping boy, thinking this is Miles' twin brother, agrees to take a message. Guards discover Miles while he is waiting and, when searching him, discover the notes Edward had written earlier. Thinking they have discovered another claimant to the throne, a guard takes the notes inside, then returns and escorts Miles to the king. When Miles realizes Edward is the true king, he sits in his presence. King Edward then assures the court that Miles has a right to sit in his presence and tells the court of the service Miles has rendered to him. pp. 212-217)*

2. Examine the denouement. Apply the adage, "What goes around, comes around" to Hugh Hendon. *(King Edward VI: corrects many of the injustices he observed in the Ruffler's gang and in prison; rules for only a few years before his death; noted for mercy during the harsh times. Miles Hendon: dubbed a knight, receives title of Earl of Kent, gold and land, and the privilege of always sitting in the king's presence. Tom: clothed with quaint but rich garments; receives commendation for his actions as king; named to the chief place in the body of governors for Christ's Hospital, where boys will now have their minds and hearts fed as well as their physical needs met; is to always wear his appointed "dress of state"; receives the title "King's Ward"; lives to be an old man. Tom's mother and sisters: reunited with Tom; promised perpetual care. Hugh Hendon: stripped of all claims to the Hendon land and title; ordered to prison by the king but released because Miles and Edith will not testify against him; deserts Edith and goes to the Continent, where he soon dies. Edith: released from marriage by Hugh's death; marries Miles. John Canty: never heard from again. pp. 217-222)*

Supplementary Activities

1. Have students sketch Tom's "quaint but rich" clothing (p. 218).

2. Have students draw a caricature of Miles based on the metaphor comparing him to a "stately scarecrow" (p. 216).

28

Post-reading Discussion Questions

1. Using the graphic organizer on page 8 of this guide, analyze the characteristics of Tom Canty, Edward Tudor, and Miles Hendon. This graphic organizer can be used for any character. *(Examples: Tom—Acts: in a princely way before his tenure as prince; loves his mother; accepts his father's abusive treatment. Feels: the need to rise above his poverty, compassion for others. Says: he is not the prince. Lives: in Offal Court in great poverty. Looks: dressed in rags; wants to be clean. Others' Actions: boys in Offal Court respect him; father abuses him; mother loves and shares meager food with him; Edward—Acts: expects others to wait on him before his time as Tom; as Tom, continues to act as a prince. Feels: loved by his father; compassion toward the common people he meets; protected by Miles. Says: people must stand in his presence; he is the prince. Lives: in the palace at Westminster; different places in the countryside. Looks: royal dress; like a prince; as Tom: ragged and often dirty. Others' Actions: as himself, pampered by everyone; loved by his father; as Tom, mistreated and abused; protected by Miles; Miles—Acts: protective, honorable. Feels: betrayed by his brother and Edith. Says: agrees with Edward's demands; vows to return to Hendon Hall. Lives: formerly at Hendon Hall; around the countryside with Edward. Looks: handsome, noble bearing. Others' Actions: at Hendon Hall, manipulative and deceptive; Edward looks to him for protection.)*

2. Using the graphic organizer on page 9 of this guide, discuss feelings of other characters. *(Examples: King Henry VIII: Frustration—"Edward" can't find the Great Seal; Anger—toward anyone who opposes him; Fear—of his son's madness; Humiliation (n/a); Relief—"Edward" answers the question in Latin. John Canty: Frustration—"Tom" seems mad; Anger—Tom comes home empty-handed; Fear—after he kills Father Andrew; Humiliation—Tom escapes; Relief (n/a). Father Andrew: Frustration—children don't want to learn to read and write; Anger—John Canty abuses Tom; Fear— John Canty turns on him; Humiliation (n/a); Relief—Tom occasionally gets away from his father. Earl of Hertford: Frustration—"Edward" seems to have lost his memory; Anger—St. John speaks of Edward's madness; Fear—Edward's inability to function as before; Humiliation—King Edward VI cautions him that he could lose his title of Duke of Somerset; Relief— the Great Seal is found.)*

3. Using the graphic organizer on page 10 of this guide, evaluate the attributes of various characters. *(Examples: Tells the truth: Does—Tom, Edward, Miles, Father Andrew, Blake Andrews; Doesn't— John Canty, Tom's grandmother, the hermit. Keeps promises: Does—Tom, Edward, Miles, Elizabeth, Father Andrew; Doesn't—the hermit, John Canty. Considers consequences of actions: Does—Miles, Earl of Hertford, Tom's mother, Blake Andrews; Doesn't—members of the gang, Tom, Edward, Henry VIII. Sacrifices for others: Does—Father Andrew, Miles, Tom, Tom's mother, Nan and Bet, the peasant family; Doesn't—Henry VIII, Edward, the hermit, members of the gang, John Canty, Tom's grandmother, Hugh Hendon. Listens to others without prejudging them: Does—Tom, Miles, Tom's mother, Father Andrew; Doesn't—Henry VIII, Mary. A good person: Is—Tom, Edward, Miles, Father Andrew, Elizabeth, Lady Jane Grey; Tom's mother, Nan and Bet, the peasant family, St. John, Earl of Hertford, Blake Andrews; Is not—John Canty, Tom's grandmother, the hermit, Hugo, criminal members of the gang. Kind and caring: Is—Miles, Tom, Tom's mother, Nan and Bet, Elizabeth, Lady Jane Grey; Is not —Henry VIII, the hermit, John Canty, Tom's grandmother.)*

4. Using the graphic organizer on page 11 of this guide, discuss the plot development. *(Setting/Main Characters: England, 1547; the protagonists—Tom Canty, Edward Tudor. Statement of the Problem: Tom, the pauper, and Edward, the prince, each accidentally assumes the other's identity. Their problem is to correct the mistake. Event 1: Tom and Edward are born on the same day. Tom, unwanted, enters a life of severe poverty and abuse. Edward, greatly welcomed, lives in the palace and has servants to meet every need. Event 2: The two boys meet accidentally and realize they look exactly alike after exchanging clothes. Event 3: Edward encounters difficulties as Tom, including abuse from John Canty and mistreatment by many. He is rescued by Miles Hendon, who becomes his protector. They roam the countryside and experience many challenging events. Event 4: Tom is thrust into the role of prince, then King of England. He learns to conduct himself as royalty and makes wise decisions. Event 5: Edward reappears on Tom's coronation day. Solution: With Tom's help, Edward proves his true identity and is crowned King of England. Story Themes: Monarchy and democracy are contrasted through the experiences of both boys. Loyalty is portrayed through Miles Hendon and those who help Tom in his role as king. Various problems of mistaken identity are portrayed.)*

5. Using the graphic organizer on page 12 of this guide, discuss the elements of the novel. *(Characters, main: Tom Canty, Edward Tudor, Miles Hendon; minor: John Canty, Father Andrew, Tom's mother, grandmother, and sisters, King Henry VIII and members of the royal court, those whom Edward meets as he roams the countryside. Setting: England, 1547. Conflict: the two boys as they face problems in their mistaken identities; characters vs. England's societal class system; Miles vs. Hugh; monarchy vs. democracy. Possible Themes: loyalty, mistaken identity, monarchy vs. democracy. Point of View: third person omniscient. Genre: fiction, satire. Author's Style and Tone: narrative, entertaining.)*

6. Using the graphic organizer on page 13 of this guide, analyze the cause and effect in the novel. *(Examples: Tom and Edward exchange clothes—cause. Each must assume the identity of the other—effect. John Canty kills Father Andrew—cause. The Canty family must leave Offal Court—effect. The Canty family gets separated—cause. Miles Hendon rescues Edward—effect. John Canty recaptures Edward—cause. Edward must join the gang of ruffians—effect. Edward is arrested for stealing a pig—cause. Miles Hendon rescues him—effect. The hermit discovers Edward is King Henry VIII's son—cause. He plans to kill the boy—effect. King Henry VIII dies—cause. Tom becomes king—effect. Tom begins to make wise decisions as king—cause. The court applauds and admires him—effect. Edward reappears on coronation day—cause. Tom helps him prove his true identity—effect. Edward becomes king—cause. He rewards those who helped him—effect.)*

7. Examine Edward's various experiences, his treatment by those involved, and any resolution he makes because of the encounter. *(The orphans at Christ's Church: mock and abuse him; set their dogs on him; resolves that, when he is king, he will provide teachers for them. The Canty family: John and the grandmother—beat him, force others to mock him; Tom's mother and sisters—comfort and console him; resolves that his father the king will repay the kindness. Miles Hendon: rescues, protects him; resolves to repay his loyalty. The gang: mock him, force him to beg and steal, the Ruffler protects Edward from John Canty, some treat him kindly; later restores the farmer who had lost his land because of King Henry. Peasants—treat him kindly, feed him. The hermit: at first welcomes him but becomes vindictive and plans to kill him when he discovers that Henry VIII is his father. As a prisoner for stealing a pig: judge treats him fairly; woman has compassion on him. As a prisoner because of Hugh Hendon: the Baptist women treat him compassionately; he is*

heartbroken when he sees them burned to death; resolves to sweep all unjust laws from England's statute books.)

8. Examine how Tom rises to the stature of a king but Edward does not lower himself to the stature of a beggar. Analyze what this reveals about both boys. *(Tom: demonstrates honor and wisdom in his dealings with prisoners, with the whipping boy, and with matters of the court. Although he enjoys the luxuries of a king, he never mistreats anyone and is appreciative of the help he receives. His actions reveal his innate desire to be good, his education from Father Edward, and his sense of right and wrong. Edward: although forced into a life of poverty and miserable conditions, he maintains his royal bearing in all situations. He honors those who help him and resolves to change the injustices he observes after he regains his throne. This reveals that he never forgets his training as a future king, yet he gains a sense of justice through his own suffering.)*

9. Analyze the importance of Father Andrew. *(Because he cared for Tom as a child, offering him a place of refuge and an education, Tom is able to fulfill the role of a prince and ultimately a king. Father Andrew's kindness is reflected in Tom's dealings with people of all ranks.)*

10. Analyze the different titles applied to Edward and to Tom. *(Edward: actual title, Prince of Wales, indicating the first in line to the throne when King Henry VIII dies. Other titles: Prince of Limitless Plenty because he has always had more than enough materially. Foo-foo the First, king of the Mooncalves, a title of mockery from the gang, which then robes him in a tattered blanket and crowns him with a tin basin; he cries tears of shame and indignation. Miles calls him "the lord of the Kingdom of Dreams and Shadows," depicting what he has thought to be a poor child's dreams of grandeur. Ultimate and authentic title: King Edward VI. Tom: Prince of Poverty and Prince of Pauperdom, indicating his princely bearing and actions even though he is poor and has no chance of becoming a true prince. Edward gives him the title of King's Ward, indicating that he will be perpetually honored and cared for in the king's court.)*

11. Discuss stereotypes of socioeconomic classes today, e.g., people who live in the "projects" or the slums, and compare with those in the novel. *(Responses will vary.)*

Post-reading Extension Activities

Note: Instructions for extension and final assessment activities are directed toward the students.

Writing

1. Write, from Mrs. Canty's point of view, the scene where she sees Tom in the coronation procession.

2. Write a poem about someone you know who has the same attributes as Miles Hendon.

3. Write a diamente poem contrasting Prince and Pauper. Pattern—Line 1: one word (Prince); Line 2: two words (adjectives describing line 1); Line 3: three words ("-ing" or "-ed" words that relate to line 1); Line 4: four words (first two nouns relate to line 1; second two nouns to line 7); Line 5: three words ("-ing" or "-ed" words that relate to line 7); Line 6: two words (adjectives describing line 7); Line 7: one word (Pauper). Place the poem in a diamond shape.

4. Write a short personal experience story in which you exchange places with someone you admire and would like to be.

Listening/Speaking

Play appropriate background music as you read a selection from the book to the class.

Drama

Write and stage a TV script for a segment on "England's Most Wanted" featuring John Canty, a.k.a. Hobbs, and the Ruffler.

Current Events

1. Bring to class newspaper or magazine articles about unjust forms of punishment in countries such as Afghanistan, Pakistan, China, or others. Conduct a class discussion comparing these punishments with those of 16th century England mentioned in the novel.

2. Bring to class newspaper or magazine articles about "instant millionaires." Compare/contrast their reactions to those of Tom.

Viewing

View a movie version of *The Prince and the Pauper* and present an oral comparison of the movie with the novel. Suggestions: *The Prince and the Pauper*, 120 minutes (1937); *Crossed Swords*, 113 minutes (1978); animated movie with Mickey Mouse as the prince, distributed by Walt Disney home videos (1990).

Art

1. Create a diorama of Offal Court.

2. Draw a map and pinpoint Edward's travels after he becomes "Tom."

3. Bring to class pictures of King Henry VIII and compare them with the way he is portrayed in the novel.

4. Prepare a family tree for Miles Hendon or Edward Tudor.

Assessment for *The Prince and the Pauper*

Assessment is an ongoing process. The following ten items can be completed during the novel study. Once finished, the student and teacher will check the work. Points may be added to indicate the level of understanding.

Name _____ Date _____

Student   **Teacher**

_____   _____   1. Write five review questions over the novel and participate in an oral review.

_____   _____   2. Write a two-line description of one of the characters but omit the name. Exchange with a partner and identify the character (s)he has described.

_____   _____   3. Share your completed bio-poems from the study guide with the class.

_____   _____   4. Write a review of the novel for the school newspaper. Use at least ten of the vocabulary words you learned in the novel.

_____   _____   5. Display your extension project on the assigned day. Be prepared to explain your project.

_____   _____   6. Correct any quizzes you have taken over the novel.

_____   _____   7. Participate in a vocabulary "bee" where you supply the definition of each word rather than the spelling.

_____   _____   8. Compare any activities such as character charts and story maps in small groups of three or four.

_____   _____   9. Working in a small group, prepare an acrostic for one of the themes of the novel. Share your completed work with the class.

_____   _____   10. Participate in class discussion of the types of conflict in the novel. Provide examples from the novel.

Glossary

Chapters 1–3, pp. 1-15
1. paupers (2): destitute; poor persons
2. offal (3): parts cut out in preparing a carcass for food; trash
3. rabble (4): crowd of vulgar, noisy people; mob
4. mendicancy (5): begging
5. melancholy (7): sadness, dejection, gloom
6. obeisance (7): obedience, respect
7. mien (12): bearing or look; appearance
8. raiment (12): clothing
9. cudgel (13): short, thick stick

Chapters 4–6, pp. 16-35
1. prodigious (16): immense, enormous
2. plebian (18): one of the common people
3. patrician (20): person of noble birth; aristocrat
4. menial (21): a servant
5. palter (29): bargain; deal evasively
6. distemper (31): disordered state of mind or body
7. stripling (32): a youth

Chapters 7–9, pp. 36-46
1. vagaries (37): whims; unaccountable proceedings
2. eccentricity (38): irregularities; odd behavior
3. panoply (39): full suit of armor
4. halberdiers (43): combined spears and battle axes

Chapters 10–11, pp. 47-61
1. mummeries (48): actors in a silent show
2. wenches (49): girls considered as belonging to the class of workers and peasants
3. commiseration (50): compassion, sympathy
4. canker (54): anything that eats away, destroys, or corrupts
5. usurper (55): one who wrongfully seizes something
6. limpid (56): clear, transparent
7. rapier (59): light, pointed sword for thrusting only

Chapters 12–13, pp. 62-78

1. waif (62): homeless child; orphan

2. inane (64): empty, silly, foolish

3. soliloquizing (66): talking with oneself

4. insolent (67): insulting, disrespectful

5. alacrity (67): quickness, alertness

6. suborned (70): bribed to do evil

Chapters 14–16, pp. 79-106

1. obsequies (83): funeral rites or ceremonies

2. preamble (83): introductory part; preface

3. ducal (84): of or relating to a duke

4. formidable (97): to be feared; dreadful; overpowering

5. veneration (103): giving reverence, especially to the aged; adoration

Chapters 17–18, pp. 107-126

1. rue (108): to regret; feel remorse

2. truculent (110): fierce; inclined to fight

3. blasphemy (113): profane, irreverent talk

4. ironical (116): mocking, ridiculing

5. epithets (119): adjectives expressing a quality or attribute; name full of meaning

6. Providence (121): divine guidance; destiny

7. uncanny (122): weird, mysterious

8. pungent (123): biting, irritating

9. kine (126): cows

Chapters 19–22, pp. 127-151

1. comely (127): fair, pretty

2. sagacity (130): shrewdness, wisdom

3. magnanimous (131): generous; above resentment

4. judiciously (134): sensibly, appropriately

5. patriarchs (136): fathers and men who rule families; venerable old men

6. archangel (136): angel of the highest order

7. impotent (141): powerless, ineffective

8. complaisance (142): willingness to please; respect

9. copse (143): a thicket of small trees or bushes

10. mortification (147): embarrassment, humiliation

11. infamous (149): disreputable, shameless, bad

Chapters 23–26, pp. 152-172

1. consternation (154): terrifying sense of disaster; dismay

2. decorum (159): appropriate behavior

3. flogging (155): beating publicly with a whip or stick

4. undulation (161): movement, as in waves

5. leal (165): loyal, faithful

6. imperviously (169): impenetrably, inaccessibly

7. miscreant (171): wicked person

Chapters 27–29, pp. 173-189

1. taciturn (173): reserved; habitually silent

2. seditious (176): stirring up discontent and rebellion

3. vagabond (183): having no fixed dwelling; wanderer

4. pillory (183): frame with holes for head and hands in which the offender was confined and exposed to pelting and ridicule

5. sardonic (185): bitter, scornful, sarcastic

6. fortitude (185): courage in adversity and pain

7. evanescent (188): fading away

Chapters 30–32 pp. 190-212

1. salaaming (191): respectful bowing

2. penury (192): want; extreme poverty

3. vassals (192): holders of land by feudal tenure

4. rent (193): tear, rip

5. largess (195): money or gifts scattered on an occasion of rejoicing

6. effigy (196): image, likeness

7. eulogistic (196): praising highly; commendatory

8. transept (201): the shorter part of a cross-shaped church

9. apparition (203): a supernatural sight or thing; a ghost or phantom

10. fealty (204): fidelity of a vassal to his lord; faithfulness

11. dynasty (205): line or family of hereditary rulers

Chapter 33–Conclusion, pp. 212-222

1. musings (213): dreamy meditations

2. torpid (218): sluggish, dormant

3. benignant (222): favorably inclined; agreeable; congenial